BEEN THERE, SEEN IT, DONE IT!

Words by John M Snell
Illustrated by Justso James Ridington

Published 2010 by arima publishing

www.arimapublishing.com

ISBN 978 1 84549 467 4

Printed and bound in the United Kingdom

Typeset in Garamond 12/16

Swirl is an imprint of arima publishing.

arima publishing
ASK House, Northgate Avenue
Bury St Edmunds, Suffolk IP32 6BB
t: (+44) 01284 700321

www.arimapublishing.com

Back cover photograph of Justso James courtesy of Lady Lou Photography
www.ladylouphotography.co.uk

John and James would like to say a big thank you to their wives,
Sharyn and Marlene, for their encouragement and patience
during the production of this book.

Contents

My shed 7

Fallen star 11

The post 13

Leftovers 19

Working from home...21

Let me out..25

Lost 29

The toilet seat 31

Thomas the tight fisted towel machine 35

Bressingham..39

A little lamp post..43

The dentist 47

Pants..49

The bottle bank 53

The royal flush..55

Little rabbit 59

The fat TV 61

A tail of two halves..63

Johnny one shoe...67

Unlucky, hey! 69

An "S" day 73

The willow tree...74

I always finish last 77

The love sick sweeper 79

Buttons 83

The wedding 85

Golf..89

Home...91

Patience 95

The complete package...97

Shoelaces 101

The appointment...105

Manners 107

Comfort..111

Potholes 113

Changing 117

6 til 9 119

Hungover 122

Another John...124

Workaholic robin 127

Do you really have to go? 129

Percy's secret pigs 133

Decisions..137

D day DIY 139

The STOP GO man 143

My eyebrows...145

Childhood 149

Felixstowe 151

House for sale...157

On sweet 159

Watch out...165

Gas attax...167

Slim Jim 171

Pure genius..173

Unforgettable love 177

MY SHED

There have been so many books written about a man and his shed but in this rhyme one ends up feeling sorry for the guy, who appears to have had a communication breakdown with his wife and the shed is his escape. This is not always the case as some wives are quite happy to get rid of their husbands for the odd hour and for the husband its return to childhood time:

My name is Ed and I own this shed
Everything's here apart from mi bed
But I've got a feeling that won't be long
Cos everything I do appears to be wrong

She jumps down my throat at the slightest word
Shouts so loud all the neighbours have heard
Garden is littered with pots and pans
Knives and forks and full tin cans
Which have missed me on the times when I've fled
To the safety of mi garden shed

Rumours are rife across the town
I'm really depressed, it's getting me down

Went to the doctors yesterday
To see what he could do
Not a lot was his reply
What you've got is nothing new
He said it's all to do with mi wife's thumb
And the pressure she applies
In my case she must push down pretty hard
Cos it brings tears to mi eyes

The only thing I know about sex is
I think it comes before seven
I've no more chance of getting that
Than I have of going to heaven

Her in doors says she's in her change
I must say she could have fooled me
She's been like it ever since I met her
In 1943

I don't expect to see any improvement
So for now, I'm just sitting in here
At least it's calm and peaceful
And I've got rid of the pain in mi ear

I'm here in all weathers, whether it snows or it rains
You'll find me here amongst all mi trains
My idea of heaven if you ask me
Better than anything on the TV

These four walls, my domain
The only thing that keeps me sane
Although her in doors is never let in
I do allow her to empty the bin

Now much has been said about a man and his shed
And let me tell you I know it's all true
Cos if anything ever happened to mine
God knows what I would do!

My Shed

Fallen Star

FALLEN STAR

In the majority of cases seeing stars of bygone years still performing can be very inspiring. There is the odd one, however, who really needs to retire! This is a message to such a person:

One concert too many
One song too long
Forlorn figure
Relying upon
Things of the past
When at his peak
Wasted fortune means he has to seek
People with memories
Who don't want to let
Bygones be bygones
To move on and forget
When times in their memory
They think were the best
Overcrowded concert
In jeans and vest
Arms raised high
As anthems ring out
No singing voice
But one that can shout
At the slightest encouragement
From their hero of old
Whose hair has gone walkies
And can barely hold
His old Fender Strat
Battered and worn

His yesteryear jeans
Stained and torn
His voice a victim
Of passing years
But from his devoted fans
Still flow the tears
But both he and they know
He's well past his best
And think he should consider a well earned rest
No longer to be seen in such a place
But retire, whilst he can, with dignity and grace

THE POST

The bible quote on my calendar says "The Lord Almighty says "Give careful thought to your ways". Divine advice? Please read on!

Oh I do really like opening the post
But my wife says I've got it wrong
I shouldn't open other people's
Because I think it's been there too long

She's nicknamed me Pinochio
And says my nose is two feet long
Because I'm always sticking it
Where it doesn't belong

There's so much excitement and joy around
Every morning the mail drops on the mat
I rush from the shower in my birthday suit
Looking like a drowned rat

Hardly able to contain myself
I shout the postie a loud " thank you"
Whops, forgot to draw the hall curtain last night?
As I stare at the postie, she's new!

Hope I don't get reported as a flasher
Because that would ruin my day
If the magistrate called me a perv
And has me put away

Back to the opening of the post
I do it at the breakfast table
Wife sits there, doesn't say a word
And I'm so excited I'm unable!

I first sort the mail into three piles
The junk, myself then the wife
I can tell by the way you're listening
You think I don't have much of a life

On the contrary my dear friends
I'm having the time of my life
But must confess I'm most looking forward
To seeing a smile on the face of my wife

She doesn't smile or say a word
Until she's had her cereal and tea
Although she may lift her eyes and scowl a few words
Like "Is there anything for me?"

Finished sorting I sadly realise
There appears to be nothing for me
Think about opening the two for the wife
Behind the paper, so she can't see

Before this though I turn to the junk
As always it's the largest pile
I hand some across the table to the wife
Who's still not managed a smile!

That appears to have been a wrong move
As a holiday brochure she sees
Two weeks for the price of one
On some place called Belize

Normally I do a second sort
Before I let her see
Anything that involves spending money
Cos we're broke, her and me!

I tell her the holiday has been booked
It didn't take long to arrange
Cos we go to Skegness every year
But I sense she's looking for a change

I sift through my pile of junk
I find things being offered on the cheap
But still we can't afford anything
So I throw them on the heap

Yes my friends the heap's so large
I can hardly get out of the door
I've written to the Royal Mail many times
Asking them to send no more

As her indoors finally opens her mail
I see excitement in her eyes
She jumps up from the seat and does a jig
She's won a Premium Bond prize

As I'm glancing up towards the cheque
I could hardly believe my eyes
She's won a measly fifty quid
Wow! What a wonderful surprise!

We'd need three more noughts on the end
To help us in our plight
I want to get rid of the cat and dog
But that always ends in a fight!

Well here ends another day opening the post
We don't appear to have any more
And what started as the height of pleasure
Ended up a total bore!

The Post

Justso James
©Ridington

Leftovers

LEFTOVERS

Isn't it great when you finally find the time to clear up the garage? There are things everywhere! The garage and the loft are the places we put things that "might come in useful". When we moved to Bury I noticed the loft entrance was very small. I was so pleased about that because it restricted what could go in there. That was a bit premature however, because we still didn't throw them away – we just put them in the garage! "Clearing up" should be changed to "moving"! That's all we do because "it might come in useful some day!" That day is the day after we've thrown it away!

I've been here for 15 years
I'm a leftover tin of paint
Sitting on this dirty shelf
Useful, I ain't!

My owner ordered far too much
Got no use for me
Although he takes me down each year
I'm put back, as you see
To gather dust on a higher shelf
Alongside an incontinent elf

Every time he laughs he wees
And we both get soaked
The other side there was an ugly frog
Who farted when he croaked!

But I soon got rid of him
I pushed him off the shelf
Next time when he's not looking
It'll be that bloody elf

But for now I've bought him incontinence pads
But couldn't get any that fit
Made him lose his balance
Every time he went to sit

I know one day I'll disappear
Up the council yard
But that'll be in some years hence
When my paint is hard

Cos owners have to make a call
For council to come out
But how will they ever do that
When they're never about

So for now I'm up here on this shelf
Got rid of frog, got rid of elf
I'm here in the fresh air and the dry
Wondering why oh why, did my owners buy?
Enough to paint the flaming sky

WORKING FROM HOME

With modern technology and laptops more and more people are working from home. Sometimes it's not as attractive as it sounds! Read on;

Next week I'm going to work from home
House needs a lick of paint
Wife's away, I'm looking after the kids
No wonder they call me a Saint!

I only painted the house last year
But thanks to the birds and the sun
I've got to redo the whole damn lot
Not my idea of fun!

Oh no! The cat has caught the budgie
When are we likely to see that?
Probably like everything else
He'll bring it up on the mat

Got to take the dog to the vet
Youngest daughter, little dear!
Found one of my old golf tees
And stuck it up his rear

Have to get the washing in
Oh no! It must be rough at sea
Seagulls have left their messages
On what they had for tea!

Have to do it all over again
What the heck do I do?
Oh damn, I've put a red jumper in with the whites
That'll cause an argument or two

Better do some cleaning now
Bathrooms, we have two
Youngest son is really helpful!
Stuffed my mobile down the loo

What's oldest son doing out there?
With that cricket bat
Appears to be hitting for a six
The next door neighbour's cat

To be frank I'm not really bothered
Our neighbour, he's got two
They're always in our garden
Using it as their loo

I know they have to do it
But the odd stone puts them on guard
And acts as a careful reminder
Not to do it in our backyard!

Now what else have I got to do?
Where the dickens is my list?
I feel like going down the pub
And getting totally..... Drunk!

Dear colleagues, I think I'll change my plans
It's pretty clear to me
That working from home, with a load of kids
Is not all it's cracked up to be?

Working From Home

Let Me Out

LET ME OUT!!

I'm sitting in church clearly not listening to a thing the Minister is saying. My mind is occupied by a rather bizarre subject in as much as I am my old saxophone shouting to get out of the case where it was put in 1974 when I finished playing in my band.

You put me here in '74
And, just because you didn't want to play anymore
You have left me cooped up in this case
To continue your part in the human race

As for me I'm left in the dark
And forced to embark
On years of silence
Years alone
Stuck up in this attic
Case covered in dust
And although I'm dry and warm, I'm beginning to rust
My pads are hard, my mouthpiece worn
My crook is dented, my strap is torn
In fact I really need an MOT
But I know that's not likely to happen to me

At least you did clean me down before you put me away
But I have to say
You cared more for that girl you were with
Attractive and slim
But still had to squeeze into the dress she was in!

Dark brown eyes and beautiful complexion
She just flashed her eyes in your direction
For you to go running to say hello
In your anxiety to get to know
You stood me down
In the corner of the stage
It seemed to me you took an age
To chat her up and say goodbye
Before you wiped me clean and dry

Oh how I remember those crazy nights
Up there on the stage, in front of the lights
Forgive me if I thought the screams were for me
But you see
I was the one making the sound
You're just full of words, not a note to be found

And all those stars I was able to meet
The little known and the elite
From Pink Floyd to Status Quo
Cliff Bennett to the Freddie Mack Show
Peter and Gordon, the Barron Nights
Then I recall those scary fights
But through them all you looked after me
But could it be?
At the back of your mind you had the HP?

Top of the Pops, Opportunity Knocks
Corn Exchange blues, the Dorothy rocks
Streets full of people at two in the morning
Arriving home as a new day was dawning
Greet the milkman up the drive
Somewhat surprised to see us arrive

When all's said and done I had my fun
And consider fifteen years a good run
But I'm fit enough to go on for a century or two
So, could it be if it's not with you,
There's someone else to hold me tight
And take me off into the night
Thus displaying my full potential
Instead of this case turning residential

Lost

LOST

Is it just me who wakes up in the middle of the night to answer a call of nature and then, in the darkness, become totally disorientated! You stagger around half asleep and trying your hardest not to put on the light because you don't want to wake up the wife. Because you can't see, you walk into every conceivable piece of furniture, cursing silently, as if it heard you. One would think if it's your bedroom you should know your way around in the dark but it's not as easy as that! In the end you make so much noise walking into things that the wife awakes and asks "What are you doing?" After hearing you grunt back "What does it look like, flying a plane?" she proceeds to point out that we're "not at home". "We've gone away for the weekend" Remember! We are in a hotel, and the toilet door is over there. Tell me, what is it like to be clever?

> *Up in the night, for a nature call*
> *Not quite awake, can't see anything at all.*
> *Everything's black, as black as can be*
> *And in walking around I knock my knee*
>
> *Who on earth put that dressing table there?*
> *Wife's asleep, so it's OK to swear*
> *I call it something else beginning with B*
> *Apologies! But mine ended with D*
>
> *I try my hardest not to turn on the light*
> *Don't want to give the wife a fright*
> *I remember she got one on our wedding night*
> *But that was nothing to do with the light, but the sight!*

I limp around feeling my way
Like Long John Silver on a bad day
Very soon the nature call turns to a plea
As I become more desperate for a wee!

Who put that wall, where there used to be a door?
I really don't know what I'm doing anymore
But the pain below reminds me of my plight
And why I'm out of bed in the middle of the night

Then I remember the door's not on that wall
That one leads into the hall
Finally brain engages, just as well
To discover I'm not at home, I'm in a hotel!

THE TOILET SEAT

I have heard it from a very reliable source (my wife) that the most irritating thing I do is leave the toilet seat up. Well she will be pleased to read on and find out the problem this poor chap had!

Sorry guys! But must take my leave
I really must make a dash
I've been drinking here for best part of the day
And am desperate for a slash

Charge down the corridor, just like a bull
But alas I see the urinals full
Check the cubicles, relieved to see
Just the one available for me

I step forward, start to relax
Then have one of those panic attacks
As the bloody seat will not stay up!

I try it, and then I try again
All the time midst increasing pain
Try to hold it up with my right hand
But everyone, you've got to understand!

I have no control of my left hand
I may have mentioned before
Well this time was no different
And I pee'd all over the floor

Tried putting one foot on the side of the pan
Using my leg to hold up the seat
Lost my balance and it went everywhere
But I'm too desperate to admit defeat!

I then tried putting both feet on the pan
Facing the cubicle door
Before I remembered I'm no good with heights
And fell arse over head on the floor!

Now I spot more pressure
By this time I'm close to defeat
He's standing menacingly by the door
Waiting to use the seat!

Just then I come up with a stroke of genius
You chew it, it's sticky and sweet
I take the chewing gum from my mouth
And stick it on top of the seat

By pushing it back to the cistern
The seat is held upright and true
Move over Mr Krapper
And become JOINT inventor of the loo!

The Toilet Seat

Justso James
© Ridington

Thomas The Tight Fisted Towel Machine

THOMAS THE TIGHT FISTED TOWEL MACHINE
(Men only)

Don't you just love it when you visit the loo, wash you hands, then come upon one of those towel machines where the clean part is so small you dislocate both arms trying to dry your hands. Either that or it gets stuck and you end up drying your hands on the part the last 100 guys used. Finally you give it a tug and discover the towel has finished! Stop moaning, big brother is watching you!

I'm Thomas the tight fisted towel machine
You'd be surprised where I have been
But for now I'm hanging on this wall
Watching you all, pay a call

You'd be surprised what I can see
When you come to have a wee
Sneaking a look at the guy next door
You end up peeing on the floor
Good grief, he's got one a foot or more!

And I can see by the look on your face
It puts your JT in disgrace

Now most of you are pretty keen
To give your hands a thorough clean
But some of you seem to forget
Have you come across them yet?
They just wave at the tap and soap
Imagining they're the Queen or even the Pope

There are those of you who live in hope
Moisten the hands, miss the soap
Don't know why you're satisfied with that
Particularly after where you've just sat

You put your germs all over the door
God knows what you've put on the floor
As you endeavour to get the highest of the day
And shower the guy next door with the spray

Now these days I have to try to compete
Against the inferior and the elite
Hot air machines of all types and sizes
They're on the wall in many guises

Automatic, buttons to start
Some so old they're falling apart
Others that have lost their thrust
Showing signs of age and beginning to rust

Some on full, but most on low power
With these you have to stand there an hour
In the end you look to other means
And end up drying your hands on your jeans!

Some have the power of a jet engine blast
These can dry your hands real fast
But take care or your hands will end up on the floor
Or possibly beat you to the door

They won't catch on if you ask me
People prefer things how they used to be
But they could improve on my model, no doubt!
By giving me a voice, so I can shout
At all those guys who've just been
And don't give their hands a jolly good clean

Bressingham

BRESSINGHAM

If it comes to taking grandsons out for the day Bressingham Steam Museum is always first on their list, in spite of the number of times they have been there. It's 27th August 2009, and we're on the end of the school holidays. D stands for Dylan and O for Owen. You will discover that not everything goes without a hitch:

We're on our way to Bressingham
It was the pick of the bunch
We leave home mid morning
And arrive there just before lunch

It's D and O's favourite place
They've visited many times
The journey there's mostly enjoyable
Spent singing nursery rhymes

But "Will we soon be there?" could be heard from the rear
Five minutes after getting in the car
A stream of "porky pies"
Came in response to their cries
As we tell them that it's now not very far!

"Want a wee - wee!"
Sung in close harmony
A crafty plot to get the car to stop
So we wave those following past
And hope this stop will be the last
As they proceed to kill off a farmers crop!

Several miles without a peep
They've both gone off to sleep
Oh damn! I think we're nearly there
Dare we disturb, dare we wake?
And end up with earache
Cos they can be quite a noisy pair

We're in luck, they wake up
Just as we go to park the car
And are both in quite a happy mood
But we overlooked the sign
And completely forgot the time
When they both needed their supply of food

Without more ado
We rush and join the queue
But soon the moans and groans start to flow
"I'm hungry", "I want a drink"
"What's that horrible stink?"
"Someone here must surely need to go!"

It takes about an hour
To make up their minds
As to what it is they really want to eat
Apparently our suggestion
Gave them indigestion
But not the things that tasted very sweet!

Minds made up
We head towards a table
Adjacent to an indoor water pool
Where people put coins in
"O" took them out
Putting them all in his pocket, he's no fool!

Meal time swiftly over
"D" heads for the carousel
That's obviously the first thing on his mind
We all climb on
But the wooden horse I sat upon
Was rough and gave me splinters in my behind!

Next stop is the fire engine
They were clearly thrilled to bits
As they sat there impersonating "Fireman Sam"
They kept on ringing the bell
Sending everyone's ears to hell
And quite clearly couldn't give a damn!

Next came a ride on the train
As it just starts to rain
They thought they had died and gone to heaven
The driver and guard
Made their jobs look hard
Both must have been seventy, going on seven!

Next came a walk around the gardens
A treat for Nan and Gran but
At this point "D" and "O" were rather choked
Until they found a switched on hose
Which they pointed at one another, not the rose
And got all their clothes thoroughly soaked

Now time is moving on
And we really must be going
The time that "D" and "O" really hate
But they came, didn't complain
Just said goodbye to train
And described their time at Bressingham as BLOOMin' great!

A Little Lamp Post

A LITTLE LAMP POST

I'm not sure to what depths I have plummeted to cause me to find inspiration in a lamp post, but if you're walking along on a dark night they do come in very useful, particularly if one has some writing to do. It's very interesting that an evening drive round the M25 (that's when you can indeed go round, and are not stuck in the queue known as the M25 car park) would cause me to notice hundreds of these lamps using up countless amounts of energy, but for what purpose? All cars have headlights don't they? Speaking of car parks, a few years ago I was travelling a lot on the M11, and for once getting good value out of my car tax with a regular shuttle down from Haverhill to Walthamstow. On one particular journey I was on my way home when I came upon a really bad traffic jam. I'm not exactly sure how long they had been waiting, but several people had taken small chairs from their car boots and were sat on the M11, enjoying the rare sighting of the lesser spotted British sun. As if this were not remarkable in itself, they were in fact sunbathing and reading their newspapers on the tarmac.

This is in fact a true story, although I don't think anyone I've told has ever believed me. If someone was there on that day I would appreciate you getting in touch with another eyewitness account. My address is "The Funny Farm"…

I'm a little lamp post
Standing in the street,
Out here in all weathers,
The cold and the heat

I help you find your way around,
By lighting up the dark
Sometimes they will use me,
Just to brighten up the park

They very seldom paint me,
But when they do its green
A colour that barely covers up
Where the dogs have been

Why is it they all head for me?
When they need the loo
I can't think of a sensible answer
Can you?

I seem to act like a magnet
To any passing dog
They have no problem tracking me down
Even in the fog

For the person who invented the poopa scoopa,
I can only give heartfelt praise
And although not everyone uses them,
I've many more fresh air days

I wonder if that same person
Could invent something for catching wee
It could take the shape of a plastic bottle
And called a "Strapalootome"

I still keep having nightmares
Of how it used to be
Choking on the smell
And drowning in the wee

There is a time of light relief
When people get it on their shoe
They adopt a rather strange walk
That's quite comical to view

They walk away with a scraping action
This rather makes me laugh
Leaving little bits of you know what
All along the path

I only see the council workers,
When my light bulb fails to action
They replace it with a new one
And then I'm the star attraction

Cos when I've got a new bulb in,
I'm shining like a lighthouse
You've gotta agree this is a vast improvement,
From being treated like a *****house!

The Dentist

THE DENTIST

Bit of fun you South Africans, we love you to bits really!

Just been down the dentist
To get my molars sorted
My guy is South African
Must have been imported

NHS is desperate
Will take what they can get
There's a strong rumour going round
Back home he was a vet

But if you're in discomfort
Crying out with pain
You're not likely to worry
From what country he came

There appears to be no difference
Between his tools and the one before
And if I remember rightly he uses
The knob on the same door
To tie the piece of string to
Having tied it to your tooth
It's probably not that different
Than removing a zebra's hoof

But even I get worried
When I have one filled or out
You should see the size of his needles
There aren't many of those about

Indeed, they're nearly 8 inches long,
And come in many styles
Hope my needle hadn't been used back home
To sort an elephant's piles

I'm sure he knows what he's doing
When he wants to knock me out
Gives me the same as a tiger
If there's ever any doubt

Hope you must have gathered by now
It's not like me to moan or complain
Cos I don't mind how he does it
As long as it takes away the pain

PANTS

Don't know where this one came from! Think it's my "little boy" naughtiness!

Do you dress to the left?
Or to the right
Do you like your pants loose?
Or like them tight

Do you like them short?
Or like them long
Do you like them plain?
Or with patterns on

Do you like those coloured?
Or like them white
Heavy material
As opposed to light

Do you pretend to be a boxer?
Or a Y
Thought about giving
Your Dad's a try?

His are quite long,
Go down to his knees
That's to prevent
A pipe work freeze

Why is it his pants all appear to be yellow?
When they started their life as white
I suppose they're showing signs of age
But I'm sure they'll be alright

I really don't mind wearing them
As long as they're reasonably clean
But that's a bit debatable
Knowing where they have been

If hard up, one could wear
Those that belong to your sister or mother
Worry yea not, they won't show
They'll always be undercover

Brand new or a few holes in
I think would be perfectly fine
But could cause a bit of embarrassment
When they're hanging on the line

No!
If you wanted my honest opinion
I'd always go with boxer, not Y's
Yes! Stick to the ones that give support
But not bring tears to your eyes!

Pants

The Bottle Bank

THE BOTTLE BANK

I still find it quite amazing how doing very mundane things can be the source of inspiration in writing. I have heard many people say they enjoy this job! Could it be ridding them of frustration?

Just been down the bottle bank
To get my weekly fun!
I take a pile of bottles
And smash'em, every one!

I pretend each one is a subject on my mind
And commence a war of attrition
With all the brown and green ones
Representing a politician

Our Gordon is quite high on the list
He's got a lot to answer for
Then comes Alistair Darling
Why isn't he shown the door?

Then, of course, there was one for Jack
Who really was the last Straw!
He's paid back fifteen hundred pounds
But how could we be sure there's no more

I work my way through the Labour Party
Til I can remember no more
I then think of other things that upset me
Such as pointless war!

I throw three bottles in for that
It really makes me mad
I throw all the bottles in gently
On the things that make me sad

Cruelty to children and animals
Are high up on the list
As are young people who damage their bodies
Partaking in drugs or get pissed!

The plight of homeless people
Has really come home to me
And, moreover, the sense of hopelessness
We see on our TV

Another bottle goes in as I remember
Those who've helped me along the way
And without that help would be nowhere
Or as happy as I am today!

A clear bottle goes in for the God I love
Because that's how it is with me
And hope others I meet are encouraged in faith
By simply what they see!

THE ROYAL FLUSH

Anybody with a history of health issues will surely have come upon this. Go on! Have a good laugh at my expense! Although it's not so funny at the time! My Professor is a real gentleman and, over the last twenty years, I've got to know him quite well. I decide to give him a copy of my book "How things were", for reasons you'll soon find out. On one occasion I was lying on the operating table awaiting the nasty deed and we were talking about one of his great loves, cricket! He was about to tell me the Test Match score, but I somehow didn't get to hear it. I wonder why?

Tomorrow I'm off for a Royal Flush
You've probably detected, I'm in no rush
To bring what's within, to the outside
I'd rather have a kangaroo ride!

The worst bit's the stuff they give you to drink
It looks and tastes like it came from the sink
After that, things can start to get risky
Unless you can run like Linford Christie

Up there's the remains of what I ate last week
As well as the occasional hard boiled sweet
At Christmas there could be a coin from the pud
But then you find out its no good
Cos since it's been there, it's out of date
A true example of the word constipate

Going to give the Professor a copy of my book
To help him understand how I really look
He's so used to staring at two fat cheeks
Two lumps and a short thing that occasionally leaks

There's always excitement about what he may find
When he's about to inspect my behind
All I pray for is what he finds is benign
I look him in the eye, it's the tell tale sign

Til now I've always been cared for
By the God I've come to know
So I hope he can be around tomorrow
When I have to go

The Royal Flush

LITTLE RABBIT

I don't know if you're like me but I really get quite upset on my drive to work as I come across dead animals in the road. The number seems to be increasing but it's so frustrating not to be able to give them a decent burial. I realise in today's fast moving society that if you stopped to try to do this you would probably end up dead as well. So this is a poem I wrote from the animal perspective.

Didn't you see me standing there?
Or was it that you just didn't care
To swerve and miss, or even brake
For my wife and children's sake

And why was it you were going so fast
This journey could have been your last
I could have been a bus or truck
Then you would have been the one out of luck

As it was, it was only me
Small but large enough to see
Blinded by your shining lights
A little rabbit without rights

If you drive that badly it won't be long
Before you join the heavenly throng
But don't worry
I'll come across and have a chat
Along with the deer, the dog and the cat

The Fat TV

THE FAT TV

Inspired by a trip to the tip! Sad init!

I'm an upset fat TV
Lying in a skip
My owner got fed up with me
And took me down the tip

It wasn't that I didn't work
Or anything
But they had to follow the Jones',
And get one that was thin

So here I am with mi mates
Out in all the cold
Although I was only bought last year,
I'm feeling rather old

I used to have pride of place
In a room that was warm and clean
But now I'm in this dirty skip
Goodness knows where it's been

It hasn't seen a lick of paint
Since I don't know when
It's covered in rust and full of holes
And then

They stack us up, right to the top
It's no fun going in first
But at least the others keep you dry
So I don't know which is worst

As for my replacement
They've hung him on a wall
It's twice as wide as I was
And nearly three feet tall

So when you walk into the room
It's like a cinema
You really have to pinch yourself
To remind you where you are

I hope you will forgive me
For being a constant moan
But my owner could only afford this
By taking out a loan
And very soon it'll be taken away
When he's lost his job and can't repay

That will be the time, I bet
When he and his family will live to regret
The day they took me down the tip
And threw me in this dirty skip

A TAIL OF TWO HALVES

You're never going to believe this! Silly season or what? After the fiasco with the condom in a meal in Switzerland, have the Americans gone one better, a snakes head!

A diner in a New York restaurant
Was unhappy, it has to be said
When he found mixed up with his broccoli,
What looked like an angry snake's head!

The diner called over the waiter
And asked: "How could this be?"
Taking a photo with his mobile phone
So the whole world could see

The head was the size of a thumb
And was a lighter shade of grey
It also had part of its spine attached
And looked in quite a poor way

Officials were unable to take details
Of how it ended up in a meal
Until the rest of it could be found
So they put out a world wide appeal

This resulted in many phone calls
Mostly, as expected, from cranks
Who said they saw the other half of the snake
Trying to withdraw money from banks

As at today, the other part of the snake
Unfortunately, has still not been found
Local police, who were called in to help with the search,
Believe it's got lost, or gone to ground

There are rumours in the city
The snake was on the restaurant's staff
And midst a disagreement with the head chef
He took a knife and cut it in half

Another story that's going round is
It was put there against its will
To keep an eye on the customer
And make sure he paid his bill!

There is also another rumour
That's quite possible, and media led
It's got a job down on Wall Street
Amongst all the others without a head!

A Tail Of Two Halves

Johnny One Shoe

JOHNNY ONE SHOE

The doorbell rings, wife is indisposed, so, although in the middle of doing something, I make my way to the door. What was it I was doing? Have a guess!

Doorbell rings
Who can it be?
Oh! It's our neighbour from 43
Exchange niceties
About the weather
"Quite cold today" I remark
"But changeable as ever"

Although she's charming
And quite discreet
I notice she keeps looking down at my feet

Curiosity wins
Downward glance
Maybe it's something to do with my stance?

Nothing that I can see

So what is it that's drawing attention?
And she's far too polite to mention
Another glance might explain
Her looking me up and down again

So I look a little longer
This time I decide to ponder
Sure enough! As I stare
On my feet there's not a pair

They don't match
They're not the same colour
Shoe on left foot
Slipper on the other

No! I didn't buy them
From one of the well known stores
And, guess what! You won't be surprised to know
I've another pair like these indoors!

UNLUCKY HEY?

Today I'm on hands and knees to find the water meter to read as we are in a new house. I found it in the end and I also found this!! Come on guys, own up! Tell me you haven't been in this situation or is it just me?

Whilst walking in the Market Square
I suddenly feel the need to dash
In the general direction of the Gents WC
And know it's for more than a slash!

I rush into the cubicle
And position myself on the seat
But notice there's no bolt on the door
And I can't reach it with my feet

I stretch out my legs as far as they'll go
Just touching the door with my feet
Hoping I've enough weight against it
And yet not fall off the seat

Another minor disaster occurs
There's no paper, but what a relief
Fishing around in my trouser pocket
I come upon a handkerchief!

I fold it neatly into shape
Knowing I'd only get one wipe
Place it between my wrinkled cheeks
And give a short, sharp swipe!

I drop the hanky into the pan
But imagine my dismay
After several flushes to get rid
The damn thing won't go away

In the end I get fed up with this
And move from the cubicle to the sink
Apologising to all those around
For kicking up such an awful stink!

I reach the sink in one piece
Despite the awful smell
I stretch to get a squirt of soap
But find that empty as well!

I resort to washing just with water
And I'm the only one who knows that
But the tap I push just slowly drips
Could easily have been a gnat!

I reach the last challenge of the visit
Having made my way to the drier
Only to see the "out of order" sign
Held on with a piece of wire!

But I hold my hands under anyway
Not the slightest breeze comes from the spout
I turn to complain to the attendant
But there appears to be no one about

So I stroll out of the WC
With guilt written across my face
Wiping my wet hands on my jeans
And disappearing at a pace

Unlucky Hey?

An "S" Day

AN "S" DAY

This little ditty is written to be recited very quickly. Try it!

Sitting out here in my short sleeved shirt
Seeking some shade in which to sit
Seeing shy, shaggy, sheep waiting to be shorn
Shirts showing shearers starting to sweat a little bit

Shortly the sheep will all be shorn
And the shearers will sit down in the shade
Sharing sandwiches made from salmon and cream cheese
Swilled down with Schweppes lemonade

It's the shearer's next job to move the shorn sheep
To a place the shorn sheep can sit
With sufficient shade from the sweltering sun
And I guess that's just about it!

THE WILLOW TREE

It's a Saturday and my wife and I have just been to do a book signing of my book "How things Were" at Henderson's in Haverhill. When we left home I asked her if she would drive. She joked and said that was because I thought celebrities didn't drive themselves to events. Not at all! The reason for me asking her was because I drive along that road every weekday and, if I drove along it on a Saturday, I would think I was going to work, UGH!!

Anyway along this particular road there is a very straight row of tall willow trees in the distance. As I was not driving I was able to look more closely and admire the grandeur of these trees.

Moving gently in the breeze
A row of upright willow trees
Standing there, firm and true
Other trees there are but few
What there are, look not so grand
Bent and twisted, upturned hand
But willow listens, hears the call
Skyward bound, straight and tall
Until one day at touch of saw
Lying where it stood before
Our willow leaves its friends and dies
Oh no! It's not a sad demise
As if before your very eyes
With craftsman's skill and sharpened blade
A thing of beauty is portrayed
Not to stand in quiet hall
But used to stroke the leather ball

No better sight or sweeter sound
To knock the ball out of the ground
To help your side to victory
And it only started as a tree!

The Willow Tree

<u>Some time later</u>
With craftsman's skill and sharpened blade
A thing of beauty is portrayed

I Always Finish Last

I ALWAYS FINISH LAST!

Firstly let me say I have a great boss! Once or twice a week he comes into my office and says "Come on John Snell! Let's go over the canteen and get you away from that VDU!" So off we trot and arrive at the canteen after the shortest of walks. Then battle commences! I have to start eating my little sandwiches as fast as I can in order to finish at the same time he does, who has food piled on his plate to the height of Everest! I always lose but it's given me this:

Most days I sit up in my office
Eating my ham and bread
Looking at news on MSN
And resting my weary head

Sometimes my boss walks in
And we both walk to the canteen
Both needing to rid our noses
Of where the cobwebs have been

He's got a healthy appetite
And by golly he really can eat fast
No matter how quickly I try to eat
I always finish last!

I used to take three sandwiches
But that was two too many
If he speeds up his eating any more
I'll end up not eating any

I'm concerned he'll end up very ill
If he continues to shovel it in
Unless he's got a cast iron stomach
Or possibly one of tin

Perhaps I should eat nothing
As everyday it keeps repeating
Should I invent an excuse for not going?
And say "I've got a meeting"

But that, I feel, would be really sad
Cos I enjoy our little talks
Perhaps I should play a little trick on him
And hide the canteen knives and forks!

THE LOVE SICK SWEEPER

We recently extended the size of our kitchen by knocking down a small study that adjoined it. As well as giving us a much larger, more workable kitchen, the new window gave us clear vision out of the front of the house for the first time. Whilst I was recovering from my cancer operation I sat in the kitchen, looked out of the window, and was pleased to see the road sweeper moving slowly along collecting all the dirt and leaves that had accumulated in the gutter. Full of praise that we, the customers of the council, were getting excellent service, nothing more was thought of the event! That is until half an hour later, when I noticed he came past again. Yes I know the road has two sides but half an hour later he came past again and continued to do so for the next two days. In endeavouring to capture this most important event, I felt a rhyme coming on!

We have a friendly road sweeper,
Benjamin is his name
He sweeps our road from dawn til dusk
What is his little game?

Up and down the road he goes
Until it begins to shine
In fact we could even eat our meals off it
Or drink a glass of wine

We suspect he's absent minded
But it could be love he's after
It could be just someone to talk to,
Perhaps a little laughter!

But people could start to complain though
If they don't know all the facts
But they're probably only concerned
If it increases their council tax

Please don't misunderstand us Benny,
We love your yellow truck
And appreciate your daily visits
To clear away our muck

But Benny, if you're not careful
You'll wear the road away
So give us a break for a wee while
And come back another day.

The Love Sick Sweeper

Buttons

BUTTONS

It's New Years Eve 2009 and, yes you've guessed it, I'm getting changed to celebrate with friends and family. It's not the first time I have had a moan about these but the first time I'm looking for your sympathy!

Oh, how I hate these buttons!
Hope they'll get rid of soon
They should be working on a replacement
Instead of going to the moon

Baby's buttons are always too small
Or I'm all fingers and thumbs
That's why I hope someone else will volunteer
When it comes to changing bums

Years ago I suggested velcro
Can't recall if in jest or what
It's a pity I didn't get it patented
As I see it's now used quite a lot

For a while men had things called fly buttons
But they were replaced by a zip
They were much better and practical to use
As long as you don't give your JT a nip

Not content with this innovation
They've gone back to buttons again
I bet the fashion designers are all female
Or maybe just plain stupid men

If one is in a hurry
They are not the best thing to have
Must allow a ten minute undoing time
When you're going to the lav

What about the buttons on shirt cuffs
Not content with one, they now have two
Totally impossible to do both up
And a marathon to undo

They've now put one in the gap in your shirt
You know the one between elbow and wrist
Never understood what the gap was for anyway
Probably where the sewing machine missed!

Well I guess I've had my moan about buttons
And you probably all wonder, of course
Convinced I'm turning into a grumpy old man
Who needs to get off his horse!

THE WEDDING

Whilst most weddings are wonderful there are those used to score brownie points over your relatives about your job, car or whatever. This is how I imagine a conversation on the latter could go!

Oh we really must come and pay you a visit!
Where was it you say you live?
I must get a pen and write it down
My memory's just like a sieve

Oh you live in Camden
I imagine that's quite a nice place
Particularly if you can get on well
With people from another race

And how many children have you got
Five did I hear you say?
You appear to have put on quite a bit of weight
Oh sorry, you're in the family way (again!)

It's one of yours picking his nose at the table
Correct me if I'm wrong
He's the one sitting at the end
Looking like a miniature King Kong!

No mistaking where he gets his looks from
He's exactly like his Dad!
Fat, scruffy with untidy hair
And behaving slightly mad

My Gordon's a Managing Director you know
And he drives round in a Merc
Has your Ernie got a job?
Or is he still out of work?

Oh and is it your car in the car park?
That's filthy and fifteen years old
With a coat-hanger where the aerial should be
Sounds like a lawnmower, I've been told

Oh and who's that girl giving my son a good hiding
Has to be one of yours!
Wearing a dress rescued from the tip
Or one of the charity stores

Last thing I heard about your oldest
He was doing six months inside
Receiver of stolen goods I believe
That he forgot to hide!

What more could one expect
He was never bright at school
In gardening was sent to buy wire netting seed
And he went, the silly fool!

My Martin is at Oxford
Training to be a doctor
Paul is in the RAF
Flying a helicopter!

Oh I don't know how you manage!
But then there's always the State
If you fill your forms in as I expect you do
You're probably on a good rate!

I have to say you look far more relaxed
Than those I have at home
Perhaps it's us who have it wrong
Cos all we seem to do is moan!

The Wedding

Golf

GOLF

In the 70's my boss and I went to the local professional for some golf lessons. I mention this because watching me you would not know that! Anyway it's now 2010 and my old group manager Geoff has invited me to play again. The first time we played I was like Tiger Woods! From then on I was in the woods!! Anyway, this one arrived as we sat drinking in the 10th hole. Why the 10th? You'll find out in a minute!

Just been for a game of golf
With my mate Geoff, what fun!
We start at eight in the morning
And get back at half past one

In that time we only play nine holes
An indication of our skill (or lack of it!)
If Geoff doesn't find himself in the rough
Then I most certainly will

He seems to have developed an awful slice
And I've got a terrible hook
In fact most of the shots we try to play
You'll not find in a book

Geoff's attraction to the trees
Reminds me of something canine
Although they occasionally come in useful
To keep his ball on line

When it comes to bunkers
Both of us are difficult to teach
And are more at home with buckets and spades
Playing on Lowestoft beach

Our fairway shots are just as bad
In fact they are a complete failure
The divots we take are all so deep
We almost end up in Australia

It's on the greens where we excel
We never take more than ten
We both seem to go past the hole
Again and again and again

As well as enjoying a little walk
We're out of the house for a while
Out from the feet of both our wives
The only time we see them smile!

HOME

Poetry Aloud are doing an "Open Mic" at Waterstones on a theme of "Home". This was written to show there is an end to this man's talent!!

No matter how far and wide we roam
There's nothing quite like coming home
Fish are dead, budgie too
Was it me or was it you
Who forgot to leave the key with number 4?
Idiot! Look! you left it in the door

Can you only think of one thing at a time?
And what's that hanging on the line
Covered in birds black and white streaks
It must have been there for the last three weeks

And why are there twenty pints of milk on the step
Was that another thing you managed to forget?
Oh, by the way, was it you?
Who was the last to visit the loo?
If it was, you were in such a rush
You came away without pushing the flush

And you forgot to give the lawn a trim
Now it's got wild animals in
I've already seen rabbits and a deer
Chased by a dog with only one ear!

And judging by the problem I had with the door
There must be three weeks papers on the floor
Surely you could have cancelled that
And can you please feed the cat
He's looking rather pale and thin
No!! Not the tin with baked beans in

Really! You are a hopeless case
And what is it you've done to your face?
Oh it's where you laid in the sun
Half like a beetroot, half like a bum

Finally, I really do think you oughta
Go to the airport and collect our daughter
Remember the one we left behind
The one you said you couldn't find
She's been arrested by the law
With a bra full of cannabis, and what's more
Her being her couldn't leave it at that
Knocked off the searching officers hat
No doubt you'll find her in a cell
I'm sure there'll be room for you as well
Or while you're there the time might be right
For you to book another flight
Where to? As far away as poss
Putting it bluntly, I don't give a toss!!

Home

Patience

PATIENCE

If you've read my book "How things were" you will have read about my lack of patience when it comes to DIY:

Oh Lord, I need some patience
And I want it now
I have some DIY to do
And I haven't got the foggiest how!

What is that I hear you say?
Use the instruction book
I think I've put it in the bin
But I'll go and have a look!

Yes the dustmen have already been and gone
It'll end up down the tip
And I don't fancy going there
And hunt for it in a skip

Starting all over again
Is the best thing I can do, no doubt!
But I've put some pieces in the wrong place
And I can't get the damn things out

I think I'll have to force them apart
And see if that will do
If they happen to break in half
There's always a tube of glue!

Nothing seems to be going right
I've broken three parts out of four
It's beginning to look like Humpty Dumpty
Laying on the floor

Thankfully my wife has gone shopping
That was a stroke of luck
But she's sure to pick up on my malaise
When she gets back in the truck!

Now back to this strange object in front of me
Supposed to be a bedroom chest
But I think it resembles a sputnik
Or a TV aerial at best

How am I going to get out of this?
Without my ear being bent in half
Suppose I could take it back to the shop
But they'll think I'm having a laugh

No! I think I'll have to own up
And take what's coming to me
She'll probably ban my trips to the pub
But that's the worst it could be!

As for the supposed bedroom chest
She'll throw it in the garden at sight
And guessing the kind of mood she'll be in
I'd better sleep in the shed tonight

THE COMPLETE PACKAGE

Don't know about you but I've never discovered longevity in materialism. My family occasionally laughs at me (in fairness more than occasionally!). You see when I get gifts at Christmas such as slippers or shirts I put them in the wardrobe for a rainy day or just for Sundays. How things have changed! When I was a lad we had "Sunday best" clothing which meant this particular outfit had one hole in as opposed to many in my weekly attire. In truth I put my new clothes in the wardrobe until my existing items are completely worn out. There I have a problem! You see, even if my slippers have holes in them I still wear them (because they're comfortable!). You can see now the problem my family have with me, but let's see how the opposite get on!

So you think you're the complete package
Better than anyone by far
With an array of the latest designer clothes
And your fast, expensive car

If you're thinking the thrill and excitement will last
I'm sorry to bring you bad news
Cos I only give it a few more weeks
Before you change your views

Why not build your life around relationships
And not around a house and a car
Because when the time comes and you need to talk
They won't get you very far

I've yet to see a house with a mouth
Or a sports car with an ear
You'd look very silly talking to them
And they're not designed to hear!

Oh, and by the way, the friends you have
They're only around for your money
You just watch! When you fall on hard times
They'll disappear, and to you it won't be funny

Remember the guy you nearly knocked down
When you were going too fast
Doing 50 in a 30
Laughing, as you went roaring past

Well that man was on his way back home
Having spent the day at the hospital
Giving comfort and hope to the sick
To you I know it means little

But the way in which you drive around
He will soon be seeing you there
And do you know what, he'll extend to you
The same attention, love and care

You see that man has a great big heart
Larger than yours by far
And I know it will be overflowing with love
For you, not your house or your car

The Complete Package

Shoe Laces

SHOELACES

My wife has just bought me a new pair of black lace up shoes, and I'm encountering difficulty doing them up. You note I said my wife bought! If it was left to me I'd still be wearing the pair I went to school in. Anyway to be helpful she came out with a load of solutions! One I definitely didn't like!

I seem to be having problems
Tying the lace that's in my shoe
You see there's a huge great lump in the way
Known as a stomach to me and you!

I doubt it's got anything to do with
The food I eat on a normal day
More likely to be the chocolates and sweets
You should see me put away!

You see, when I start to eat chocolates
I'm finding I just can't stop
Within a couple of minutes
I've cleared the layer on the top

When I used to drive to work
I was never without a sweet
In fact, I measured the distance there and back
By the number I could eat

It was three Murray Mints, four Werthers
Or five clear mints each way
But the soft fruit sweets didn't last very long
I could eat a packet a day!

I loved those chocolate caramel toffees
But they too didn't last very long
In fact, if I had any left when I arrived at work
I'd think there was something wrong

Wife says I'll have to try to cut back
In fact, I'll have to diet
She says I've got to eat more fruit and veg
OK with me if you fry it!

She says I'll have to stop eating sweets
Now that news is a disaster!
I resort to smuggling them into the car
And eating them a little faster

The other day I made a mistake
And she saw all the empty wrappers
She chased me up the garden path
And kicked me in the .....ankle!

Fish and chips on a Saturday night
She says "They'll have to go"
I still have them, when I come out of the pub
But she's never gonna know

I've been doing this now for several weeks
It appears to be working well!
I roll around in someone's bed of roses
To camouflage the fish shop smell

She drags me off to do the weekly shop
It's not a lot of fun
She's banned me from buying those lovely cream cakes
Or even a currant bun

What else is she depriving me of?
Better not go there!
Oh yes, she makes me stand a lot
She's sold my bloody chair

Its six months now I've been dieting
And I've lost just half a stone
Most days I'm like a grumpy old man
She'd have done better to leave me alone

The Appointment

THE APPOINTMENT

It's 4.30pm and I'm sitting in the waiting room at Addenbrookes Hospital awaiting a 3.20pm appointment. So I've been sitting here for an hour and a quarter with insufficient energy to do anything like reading, then all of a sudden three lines dropped into my brain. I had finished the rhyme by the time I was called. My brain had secretly put me where the receptionist was and, boy oh boy, if the outward appearance showed composure when challenged, what was going on inside was a totally different story. In fact, something like this!

I'm perspiring
You're so tiring
About what are you enquiring?
I know your time was half past three
But before you, two more we'll see

When we've done, then you can come in
But honestly, making such a big thing
One would think you're the only patient we have to see
But believe you me

We've already seen forty five today
But no one had as much to say
As you, and how long you've been waiting
Meanwhile, I've been debating

Should I move you right down to the end
And make you spend
Another hour sitting there
In your pinstripe suit and Grecian hair

You know I'm glad I'm not your wife
I doubt she has much of a life
Victim of insults and humiliation, but worse by far
She's third in line, behind your job and your car

Your kids are not even an also ran
Pretending to see them when you can
When all along you're just the great escaper
To watch the news and read your paper

If I were you I'd just chill out
Cos I'm certain there are many more people about
Whose time is far more important than yours!
But if you're still not happy
THERE ARE THE DOORS!

MANNERS

One of the things I have found in writing is that any word, any topic, any view, any emotion can be up for grabs when it comes to inspiration. Normally one wouldn't admit to bad manners but sometimes my excitement gets the better of me and I speak with my mouth full of food! As one would expect, I receive the smacked wrist from her in doors but I didn't get it for nothing! Read on:

You were speaking with your mouthful
How did you expect me to hear?
Now I've got bread stuck in my hair
And cucumber in my ear

Mayonnaise on my blouse
And what's that on my skirt
You couldn't have washed the lettuce properly
I think it looks like dirt

You really behave like a little boy
When you come to eat
I see you've dropped tomato on your tie
And potato salad on your seat

And what's all that white stuff
Laying on the table
It looks very much like salt to me
It would appear you are not able
When you put it on your food
To shake it over your plate
Rather over the whole Universe
And in a figure of eight

And look you've dropped some beetroot
On that nearly new white shirt
I doubt if that stain will ever come out
But don't suppose it will hurt

It'll blend in with all the other stains
You appear to have acquired
There's spaghetti bolognaise and the contents
Of the oil gun you've just hired

Why don't you read the instructions?
That would sound sensible to me
Looking down the barrel, whilst pulling the trigger
What did you expect to see?

Whatever it was, you got a shock
So did your face and shirt
Not too concerned about the face
But as for that flipping shirt!

It cost me nearly two hundred pound
I got it from Trotter & Dean
I've had to wash it so many times
To try and get it clean

For the future can I suggest to you
Before you do dirty jobs
You start by taking off all your clothes
And wear just a pair of clogs

That's the only way I know
Of you keeping something nice
But you don't listen to any thing else I say
So why should you this advice

Oh yes! Where were we at the start of all this?
We were talking about your manners at the table
Well I expect to see some improvement soon
Or you'll have to eat with the horse in the stable!!

Manners

Comfort

COMFORT

I sometimes squirm when I see someone's interpretation of comfort to the one I have. I think mainly of impoverished countries where they have the same meal day in day out, that is if they get one! People in Malawi travel miles on foot to a church service where I have about half a mile to go and I take the car. Would you believe it we are quite often late! Closer to home are the homeless! I started this poem, as indeed most, before I wrote this introduction so I can't claim any cleverness around the use of the word "box". It was just how it came:

If comfort came in boxes
The one for me would need to be large
I wouldn't fancy living in a tent
Or even on a barge

The latter I would have problems with
Because I'm 64, and haven't yet learnt to swim
I'd end up just like dear old "Frank Spencer"
By tripping up and falling in!

As for tents, they are different now
To when I was a boy
They now have bedrooms and a loo
And loud TVs that annoy!

What's the point of going away?
Just to experience what you have at home
It appears to me all that's missing
Is the garden, the shed and the gnome!

No! When I reflect on comfort
I think of a swimming pool and a spa
Oh yes! And of course a chauffeur
To look after my big expensive car

A celebrity chef to look after my meals
A pilot to fly my planes
A groom to look after the daughter's horses
And to plat their tails and manes

A captain for my luxury yacht
Down off St Tropez
A nanny to look after all my kids
So the wife and I can get away!

These are some of the comforts
I'd like to base my life upon
But I can tell that you can't wait to say
Dream on brother, dream on!

POTHOLES

Just been looking at MSN during my lunch break and found this amazing story! Navestock Parish Council in Essex are suggesting not filling in potholes but leaving them to act as traffic calmers. If that's not an invitation to put finger to keyboard I don't know what is!

It would appear they're using potholes
To act as traffic calmers
It's a bit like doing away with racehorses
And replacing them with llamas

I agree it's so much cheaper
For the potholes not to be filled in
Do you think that's what the council had in mind?
When they came out with this stupid thing

It's a bit like doing away with light bulbs
And say you're saving power
Why don't we save on paint?
And dismantle the Eiffel Tower

Why not do away with cat's eyes
I'm sure they would equally be pleased
Why not save on tissues
Use your hand, every time you sneeze

Why don't we save on petrol?
By pushing our cars around
And perhaps save on aircraft fuel
By keeping them on the ground!

Why not do away entirely?
With expensive holidays abroad
Send everyone to Pontins!
Oh no! Good Lord

We could do away with clothes
And run around absolutely starkers
That way we could save our neighbours
From being such nosey parkers

How about doing away with war?
And living our lives in peace
We could then do away with the Army,
RAF, Navy and Police

That would mean we don't need politicians
Who we know we can't trust anyway
We could all walk around with smiles on our faces
HIP HIP HIP HOO – bloody -RAY!

Potholes

Changing

CHANGING

I sometimes wonder if we didn't have the use of washing machines and had to do washing by hand would we be as keen to change our clothes as many times as we do. I was one of six children and I recall Monday was "wash day" and that was the whole of Monday from early morning until dark my Mum did the washing. I'm sure we didn't change as often as we do now and I don't appear to have suffered by it. Well at least I don't think I have! The fact that people don't come within yards of me has been interpreted as not wanting to invade my space. Perhaps there's another reason!

Old habits die hard and sometimes I try to wear things more than once, but get caught out! Then come all the other gripes!

"I'm sure you've worn that shirt before"
Said she, standing at the bedroom door
"It's all creased round the bottom and there's that mark"
"The pigeon made when we were in the park"

"And I can see other marks where you've dropped your food
Not wishing to be rude
But with a mouth as large as yours how can this be
You must need new specs to help you see!"

"And another thing, if you don't finish your drink
Please can you pour the rest down the sink?
And not leave as someone else's chore
Who loads the dishwasher, and pours on the floor"

"Oh by the way, when did you last clean your shoes?
I think it was when we heard the news
That we were victorious in the Second World War
Or come to think it, maybe it was the Boer!"

"What colour are they by the way?
Standing here it's hard to say
I see black, brown and shades of blue
As a result of cleaning them with the brush from the loo"

"Those trousers, you've had them on for weeks
What are those rather long dark streaks?
What? Got them on a holiday in Corfu?
But we went there in 2002!

"As for you, when did you last have a shower?
When the Liberals were last in power?
I thought so, one can often tell
When neighbours start complaining of the smell"

Don't know what your friends must say?
With you wearing the same clothes every day
Oh! They all do that as well
No wonder you can't detect the smell

Well my dear, I think I've said enough!
And will have to accept you're a natural born scruff
So be as you are, or want to be
But don't expect to be seen out with me!

6 til 9

Fellow colitis sufferers may well have these experiences. If so, laugh it off or suffer the consequences!

Oh how I hate the mornings, 6 til 9
It's the time when things are not fine
There am I staggering about
Stomach feels it's inside out

Unmade jigsaw, scrambled egg
What's that big bruise on my leg?
Oh it's what I did the day before
Walked into the bathroom door

Here am I, in such a rush
Hair gel ends up on toothbrush
Toothpaste ends up in my hair
That'll make my workmates stare!

Electric toothbrush out of power
Out comes old faithful to save the hour
Good grief! I've had this one since '98
On closer inspection it's in a right old state!

The bristles are flat and hardly clean
Not surprised, as I know where it's been!
Have often used it to clean my specs
That accounts for those little dark flecks

Parazone! Is this a mouthwash, must be new?
Hope it's not the one she uses on the loo
If it is, I've just made a terrible mistake
No wonder my stomach's beginning to ache

Must rinse the bath, remove the pubes
Clean around the toothpaste tubes
Hang the towel up, but not on the floor
Make sure you dry off the shower door

Oh dear, I have so many things to remember
No matter if it's June or December
Tablets, ID card and mobile phone
Now I'm emerging from the robot zone!

Daren't tell the wife the phone is flat
Look out!, I nearly stand on the cat!
Oh, did I remember to lock the door?
"John, how many things can your little brain store?"

"You know damn well you locked it just now
Remember! you'd temporarily forgotten how"
Oh yes! I'm on the way to work now, feeling fine
But please Lord, would you mind cancelling 6 til 9!

6 til 9

HUNGOVER

Isn't it awful when you walk around your town and find the result of someone's over indulgence laying there on the path, and you have to step into the road to avoid it!

Forgive the explicitness!

Oh, if I only had wings
To fly me away
And back to the start of another day

Cos this one's not good
I've been down the pub
Had a gutful of beer and some awful grub

Now I'm irritable, tetchy and not very nice
And probably about to pay the price
For one drink too many
One mouthful too much
My heads in two halves
Too fragile to touch

My stomach is aching
And to get to the loo
There must be no hesitating
Or between me and you

My socks will get full of my earlier lunch
And I'll be just one of a sickly bunch

There are some of mi mates,
Throwing up in the street
With a mixture of veggies,
Brown ale and meat

Oh what lessons we learn,
What price we pay
Now you know why I want to get rid of today

Hungover

ANOTHER JOHN

After a day in the office isn't it lovely when you can go out for a walk, taking in some much needed fresh air. It's better still if you meet someone, a complete stranger, and stand to have a chat. This is how I met John. A lovely guy, lorry driver by trade!

Out for a walk, came upon
Another guy whose name was John
His dog was taking him for a walk
So to give him a rest, we stopped to talk

About friends we both knew, way back in the past
And how it was he couldn't walk very fast
He suffered from high blood pressure and was way overweight
And knew very well how he got in this state!

He was a lorry driver
Who sat in his cab!
Snacked all day long
And created the flab

He went to the doctor, who
Because of his size
Suggested he should exercise

He decided to walk
His dog liked it too
Not just a few yards
But a mile or two!

So if ever you see my friend John
Whilst out on a walk
Be sure you have time
To both stand and talk

Another John

Workaholic Robin

Justso James
© Ridington

WORKAHOLIC ROBIN

It's the end of April and I'm working hard in the garden at Ixworth House. When I say garden, when I have removed the ivy and elder there will be little left. But I am feeling very encouraged as the apple trees, once strangled and overrun by ivy, are now full of beautiful blossom as if to say thank you. Our many patient hours have been rewarded. Isn't it great when you start work in the garden and within minutes a friendly robin comes to say hello!

Robin Red breast
Hunting food
With which to feed
Its hungry brood

Pin like legs
Head cocked aside
Making no attempt
To hide

It's on a mission
Has been all day
And as long as I'm around
It'll stay

To collect the worms
Which continually appear
Without inhibition
Without fear

Beak so full and overflowing
I watch, and it appears to be going
To its nest in yonder tree
Giving its youngsters overdue tea

But it's not long before its back
To carry on its vicious attack
Dissecting worms too large to carry
Mustn't linger, mustn't tarry

Backwards and forwards without ceasing
Until, hunger cries decreasing
All is quiet, all is still
Youngsters appear to have had their fill

Parents take a well earned rest
A chance to tidy unkempt nest
A chance to talk, the robin sings
Before the next session of "meals on wings"

DO YOU REALLY HAVE TO GO?

Don't you just love it when you visit friends, who perhaps you haven't seen for a while, and they continue to bombard you with photo after photo!

Pray! Please stay a little longer
Do you really have to go?
I've got all last year's holiday snaps
And of the local village show!

Remember the vicar came along
And was rather partial to bubbly
I heard by the end of the afternoon
They found him in the shrubbery

The villagers managed to bring him round
In time for Sunday morning
But it did little to improve his sermon
And the congregation was still yawning

Then there are snaps of our neighbour's black cat
Not such a pretty sight!
I took them in our garden
In the middle of the night

You can just about see the outline
As he crouches to catch a mole
Then I discovered he wasn't doing that at all
He was just filling up a hole!

Oh you must see the DVD of next door's wedding
It was a grand affair
I think it could have been better though
If the groom had washed his hair!

And trying to cover it up with a topper
Made us laugh til one saw the tears
Especially as it was far too big
And covered his eyes and ears!

I have photos of next door's parrot
It speaks to people passing by
I'll not tell you what he said to the vicar
Or his boss up in the sky

I must show you our new kitchen
Got it from MFI
It took them nearly two years to complete
Without a word of a lie

Do I see you starting to drop off George?
Or are you just resting your eyes?
No! I've been asleep for the last three hours
Is that any surprise!

Do You Really Have To Go?

Percy's Secret Pigs

PERCY'S SECRET PIGS

The Snells are busy getting ready to move to Ixworth. As I start packing boxes I think of neighbours we've had since a child. We have been truly blessed as all have been wonderful. One particular family comes to mind about which me and my brothers used to create little stories about the father. One thing that I will always remember is that he became very ill and was bed bound and I could always hear singing through our adjoining bedroom wall. Somewhat mystified I asked Mum what it was. Oh, she said, its Percy singing hymns. What a great witness that was if ever there was one? Singing your way to glory! Anyway, this was one of our stories about him:

"What's that noise coming from Percy's shed?"
I asked my Mum one day
I think she knew all along
But didn't like to say

"I think he must be doing something"
She said, rather than be upfront
"Surely someone ought to help him" I reply
"Cos I can hear the occasional grunt"

I've seen him carrying bags of something
Down the garden path to the shed
Looking like Father Christmas
Without a hat on his head

I didn't know what was in the bags
But I had a good idea
So for now I'll keep it under wraps
And go by what I hear

The grunt didn't sound that human to me
Animalistic I think
And that's another question I asked
Who's creating that horrible stink?

If it's Percy who's responsible
I'm sure the doc must have a cure
To me it smells like something familiar
Yes! More like farmyard manure

I notice he's put a light in the shed
And is out there in the middle of the night
I thought I was just having a dream
When strange noises woke me up with a fright

And why is he digging his garden?
At two o'clock in the morn
I've noticed he's always out there
But goes in just before dawn

His veggies are always superior to ours
And I've often wondered why
He has two foot long parsnips
And runner beans ten feet high

Once in a while I'm woken up
By a lorry, and a lot of grunts and squeals
Looking closer I spy four legged animals
Being loaded onto these wheels

Unless I'm mistaken, Percy
They look like pigs to me
I know the light is not very good
But good enough for me to see!

You know you shouldn't keep them
I'm sure the council will create merry hell
But don't worry, as long as the occasional leg of pork comes our way
We're certainly not gonna tell

Decisions

DECISIONS

It's a beautiful day! Quite a sharp night frost but that's already starting to melt under the warmth of the sun. I drive slowly, gazing around at the sheer beauty of God's creation. You know I think you have to have more faith to believe this just happened by chance, if you get my drift! Had two days with no inspiration, just frustration! Then all of a sudden this:

If my mind was as clear as today's blue sky
Then perhaps I might discover why
I'm charging about, shouting aloud
A solitary voice within a crowd
Decisions, decisions
So many to make
For goodness sake!
Why do I have to choose the wine?
Learn how to hang the clothes on the line
What colour to paint the downstairs loo?
Should it be green, or maybe blue?
By now I've said I really don't mind
Cos you know damn well I'm colour blind
What kind of gel to put on your hair
As long as it's kept straight, I don't care!
What type of cheese to get, Oh what a saga!
Then there's the decision on the lager
Oh and there's the card for a special friend
The choice, it stretches from end to end
I'll pick anyone, I'm sure it will do
Well it will for me, but not for you!
You linger around and look at them all
Over the speaker comes the dreaded call

The store is now about to close
But we've still got rows and rows
To ponder over, have a look at
Manager is grumpy, can be sure of that!
Trying not to notice we walk away
Suppose we could comeback another day
But her in door's just one thing on mind
We need the rolls that wipe your behind
We can't take just any old one
We need the ones that are soft on your bum
We get there, but I see her hesitate
Do we want six or do we want eight?
For goodness sake
There's no sell by date
Grab the most, it's more economical
By now we're beginning to look quite comical
As we're the last ones in the store
And still I find she wants more!
We've forgotten to get the BFP
And what are we having tonight for tea
By now the Manager's had enough
And takes both of us by the scruff
And leads us, with purpose, to where you check out
Surprised to find there's no one about
He has to work the till on his own
And by now he's going to be late home
In view of his attitude we play hard
By paying with a credit card
But as we load the trolley and say goodbye
One couldn't fail to see the sigh
He gave us as he showed us the door
Hoping we won't come back anymore

D DAY DIY

No explanation needed here, is there?

Just when I thought I had finished
She finds another piece of DIY
I've hung the contents of B&Q
And half of MFI

I've been at it since six this morning
She had a list of things to put up
Pictures, photos and towel rails
Without so much as a drip in my cup

I must say it's not like me to complain
But I'm feeling muscles I've never known
Aching arms and back, and stiffening knees
And you should see the blisters I've grown

Tomorrow's list is as long as your arm
And all of them I'd rather not do
A new plug on the iron, lamp shades to fit
Then a new seat on the loo

The last one got broken
When I stood on it to fix a pole
My standing leg took a turn for the worse
And my foot ended up in the hole

Following that she threw my slippers away
Claiming them to be unclean
She'd have thrown them out a long while ago
If she only knew where they'd been

She's coming towards me with a large heavy door
What's she expecting me to do with that?
It's to replace the one from hall to lounge
Scratched to bits by the cat

That cats more trouble than its worth
Of that I can't be more certain
And it'll end up down the stray cat sanctuary
If it keeps climbing up the curtain

Oh no! I wish I'd never mentioned them
Although I must confess they're in a mess
She's been out and bought another pair
Two hundred smackers, no less!

No! I cannot change the tap washer
It's a job where you need the know how
You wouldn't get a window cleaner to be an MP
Or a brickie to milk a cow

Come to think of it it's not a bad idea
Getting cleaners to swap with MPs
I'm sure they could do a far better job
And not bring the country to its knees

Here she comes again with a paint brush and tin
I try to hide in the loo
I came in here at half past eleven
And its now five minutes to two

My word she's got some patience
Of that you can be sure
She's still there when I decide to come out
Not with one brush and tin, but four

I turn on the telly to watch the evening news
Can't concentrate, but I try!
I then go to bed and have nightmares
About her and her DIY

D Day DIY

The Stop-Go Man

THE STOP-GO MAN

Isn't it great when you come upon this guy! I can't think of a more boring job, well, apart from accountancy! But you know, in his little world, he has a great feeling of power! Imagine if you're at the front of the queue and he has something against Mercedes, and you happen to be in one! He could let the other side go for hours because if it says STOP, stop you must! There is also the danger he could fall asleep on the job! So next time you meet this guy don't be driving a Mercedes and give him a smile.

I'm honest Joe, the STOP-GO man
Causing havoc where I can
I'm the one who has the power
Every minute, every hour

I'm a member of that motley crew
Who holds you up or lets you through
I'm the one who can define
Whether or not you'll be on time

To catch a plane or customer date
There could be problems if you're late
You might miss out if you're not on time
And be left standing at back of line

When all's said and done I'm not a bad chap
Along with tattoos and builders crack
And I know am partial to a pint or two
But so, I guess, are the likes of you

The afternoons are tricky for me
Particularly if lunch included three
I see four cars when there's only one
Or fall asleep in the heat from the sun

It still doesn't give you the right to glare
Look at your watch, and continue to stare
So next time we meet, how about a smile
Be patient if you have to wait a while

Don't do things that might upset
Cos it could be the day you live to regret
The meeting you had with honest Joe
The man in charge of STOP and GO

MY EYEBROWS

This has been a right tease by my family for many years but what can I do? I keep forgetting to ask my hairdresser to trim them back a bit! Anyway, there seemed an opportunity for a poem I couldn't refuse!

Have you noticed I've got funny eyebrows?
Got them from my Dad!
They're black and grey and curly
Just like the ones he had, as a lad

If I'm not very careful
They fall in front of my eyes
I stick them to my forehead with superglue
Pointing them to the skies

Most men's eyebrows point from East to West
But mine also go North to South
Sometimes they are apt to get so long
They've been known to reach my mouth!

Then, as well as in the way when I'm eating
They get in the way when I kiss
It's been known in the midst of a warm embrace
Wife decides to give it a miss!"

Have you also noticed, men have problems?
With hair up nose and in ear
A friend of mine is practically deaf
Tells wife he can hardly hear

Between you and I he doesn't want to
That is, hear what his wife has to say
In fact every time she goes to speak
He looks the other way!

And what about the guys with nasal hair
Out of their cavity it flows
Most men use it as an excuse
For continually picking their nose

Some guys get smart and grow a moustache
To blend in with their nasal hair
What they don't realise, they are two different colours
But they don't seem to care!

Since having trouble with my eyebrows
I've watched what women do
Some of them shave the whole lot off
And try to start anew

They get one of their kid's crayons
And draw another one in
But it's nowhere near the original
And it's usually very thin

Well I think I've milked this one to death
And so say all the cows!
There's a limit to what one can talk about
On the subject of funny eyebrows!

My Eybrows

Justso James
© Ridington

Childhood

CHILDHOOD

We've just been to see my sister in law and her husband. They are both vicars so I have to watch my p's and q's. As I was driving home for some reason my childhood came to the fore, and the first line of the following. I guess it was picture painting with words!

Over the hill and by the brook
Is where I used to sit and look
At buttercups, as a child one knew
Endless green fields come into view

Rickety barn where once we played
In many a tree, huts were made
Collecting mushrooms at crack of dawn
Field after field of ripened corn

Sight of old tractor and binder
Kind of acted as a reminder
As excitement grew at the thought
Of many rabbits being caught

As I recall it was only a thought!

I don't believe I ever caught one
But we had an awful lot of fun
Chasing til our legs dropped off
Rising dust making us cough

Occasional hare would appear
But we would get nowhere near
As it would always run uphill
Compared to him we'd be standing still
It was many yards away
And lived to see another day

Favourite horse pulling cart
Using all its power to start
As another load of sheaves goes back to yard
He knew the meaning of working hard!

Back to the brook and building dam
Til it was dry where once water ran
And sheep and cows couldn't have their drink
But we were really too young to think
Of the consequences of our actions here
But Dad reminded us with a thick ear

Soon forgotten, threshing season
And something else to give us a reason
To spend countless hours down on the farm
Where parents knew we would come to no harm
How things have changed to our dismay
Childhood is somewhat different today!

FELIXSTOWE

It's a Sunday and this morning I have led the Church Service for the first time in must be 10 years! Afterwards we decide to go to Felixstowe, as it's our nearest seaside resort and we both felt we needed some lovely sea air. Many years ago we used to tell people how lovely the Suffolk coast was. Wish we hadn't as you'll now find out:

Just driven down to Felixstowe
For a walk along the prom
Look at all these people!
Where the heck did they come from?

We've driven round an hour so far
Looking for a parking space
Seems like everyone is here
That belongs to the human race!

There are people on mobility scooters
Trying to run us down
A guy with trousers far too big
Acting like a clown

Children eating ice creams
Dropping them on their shirt
Others picking it from the path
Along with a supply of dirt!

People dipping their feet in the sea
Killing all the fish
Imagination overtime
South of France? They wish!

Pensioners sitting on benches
Eating their fish and chips
Others walking with the help of a stick
And their artificial hips

Lovers lying on the beach
In the midst of a close embrace
Where is his other hand?
It's an absolute disgrace!

Fishermen standing on the shore
They stay there through the night
Don't appear to have caught very much
But hoping that they might!

Children and their candyfloss
What a job to eat!
In their hair, on their noses
And even on their feet!

Occasional fitness fanatics
Gently jogging past
T shirt soaked in perspiration
Looking like today's their last

Others pushing wheel chairs
Of those who sadly can't walk
Policeman and ugly Traffic Warden
Stop to have a talk

Whose car is he putting that ticket on?
I do believe it's mine
Damn and blast it's the fifth time
That I've picked up a fine

I try to explain there were no spaces
His face didn't change a bit
I tried to use "I didn't have change"
At that his dynamite lit!

"If I had as many ten pounds notes
As I've heard that from the likes of you"
"I'd be able to afford a house on the Algarve
And that with a lovely sea view"

I concede defeat and we depart for home
In a mood unhealthy for all
But not for the policeman whose camera went off
And was hiding behind a wall.

I arrive home and begin to reflect
On what was an awful day!
Never again will I sing the praises of Felixstowe
And hopefully people will stay away!!

Felixstowe

House For Sale

HOUSE FOR SALE

After 18 years at Rembrandt Way in Bury St Edmunds the Snells are on the move. But what a saga to sell your house these days! If you Estate Agents think you're having a difficult time read on!

Operation house
More people, more views
Vacuum the carpets
Clean the loos

Dusting places never cleaned before
On top of the wardrobe
On top of the door

Wash out the bath
Remove all those hairs
Dust all the paintings
Paint the stairs

Wash all the windows
We can now see through
They hadn't been done for a year or two

Put flowers everywhere to make it smell nice
At least that was the Estate Agent's advice

Oh no! I think I need the loo
I'm told
"You can't go there for an hour or two
Cos it's just been cleaned
And it smells fresh and new
More than what it does after a visit from you!"

I move around my cheeks gripped tight
Putting all the rubbish out of sight
In the cupboards, in the drawers
Time to wash the dirty tiled floors

Then my thoughts turn to the things outside
Need to cut the grass
Can't remember when it was last done
I think several years have passed

Wish I hadn't left it so long
Seems to be taking an age
Finally finish, try to sit down and rest
But given the budgie's cage

"This needs cleaning and the rabbit as well
They're both creating one horrible smell"
"Is it them or is it you
Making the air in here smell like a zoo?"

I have to own up and take the blame
But by now am in considerable pain
Then the visitors come to my aid
They ring and cancel the viewing they made

With some relief and without further ado
I run towards the downstairs loo
Oh what feelings of delight
Now my cheeks can relax and stop having to fight!

ON SWEET
(English translation for French "en suite")

My wife and I are discussing project "En Suite". To do B&B in "Ixworth House" we have to equip three bedrooms with en suite bathrooms. Of course it's too difficult for us to do, me being only able to hit in a nail, and not straight at that! The first line came up in conversation and the rest followed:

A sharp intake of breath
Tells me all is not going right
The plumber has cut the pipe too short
The carpenters out of sight

It would seem he's disappeared outside
To renew his acquaintance with the weed
And I'm not unhappy at all about that
If it satisfies his need

As long as he completes the job, of course
Before he decides to die
I promise I'll be at the funeral
But he shouldn't expect me to cry

Because between you and me he gets on my wick
He's a real pain in the bum!
Walking around, only one song on mind
Which he continues to hum

It wouldn't be so bad, of course
If he could hum in tune
But the sound coming from his overweight body
Resembles that of a castrated baboon

And as for my friend the builder
Who's busy putting up the stud-walls
His jeans would appear to be far too tight
Hence the reason for the many calls

"I don't think I can bend down that far"
Could be heard midst apparent pain
His voice sounded ten octaves higher
Not Lawrence, more like Lorraine!

Now I don't want you to think the plumber's OK
Cos I don't think I'll invite him back
Although at times he did become useful
When I could park my bike in his crack
My wife was somewhat embarrassed to see
What looked like the Canyon Grand
His trousers were almost down to his knees
And he was having a job to stand

When all's said and done he got most things right
At least that's what I had been told
But when it came to connecting taps
He didn't know his hot from his cold

Of course I didn't know about this
Until I had my first shower
Turned on the hot, got froze to death
And only thawed out in an hour

As for the lazy foreman
He's just stood around drinking cups of tea
As if that wasn't bad enough
He didn't make one for me

Sparky put in an appearance
He was in a state of shock
Wife had put his trousers in the wash
So he had to wear a frock

In fairness he had been wearing them for months
And they didn't look very clean
It was hard to say what colour they were
Blue, brown or green

Poor guy, he had just come from the docs
A problem with his bladder
We had to remember to look down to the ground
Every time he climbed a ladder

The plasterer was the next to appear
He was a messy sod
He put more plaster on the floor than the walls
And he did look rather odd

They say ones ears are never level
But his were to the extreme
Occasionally he would end up feeding his ear
When he came to eat an ice cream

We started this job in ninety one
And it's now two thousand and seven
I wish they'd hurry up and get finished
Or I'll have to send their cheque from heaven!

On Sweet
(English Translation From French)

Watch Out

WATCH OUT!

I'm late and I've arrived at work quite upset. On the way to Haverhill from Bury there is a little village called Horringer. On the right hand side on a very nasty bend is a pond. On the pond are ducks that, for some strange reason, have to cross the road. They've yet to invent a "duck crossing", those zebra's always come out on top! Ducks are not the fastest movers on the ground and today I noticed one did not make it!
It's really sad to see and this can be made worse in the Spring when Mother and all her ducklings have to cross. The cutest sight but always very worrying! I remember as a child my parents kept some ducks intending them for the table. When the time came none of us could perform the horrible deed so we kept them as pets! For what follows I am spending a few minutes as a duck!

Watch out for me
I'm only small
And I know you can't
See through that wall

But coming round that corner as you did
Could have caused an accident
Or a skid

Worse than that
You could have knocked me down
In your haste to get to town

Our friends have put some signs up
To let you know we're here
But most of you ignore them
And it sometimes costs us dear!

We're only crossing the road
To go for our morning swim
Usually take the kids with me
And enjoy pushing them all in

The limit through our village
Is 30 miles per hour
But it doesn't matter how fast you're going
If we're hit with all that power

We're either squashed upon the road
Or very badly hurt
Kind passers-by take us to the vet
Having picked us from the roadside dirt

There's little our friend the vet can do
And mutters with a frown
The injuries are so bad
I'll have to put him down

Now who's going to look after my wife and kids?
After I have gone
We don't have any life insurance
On the pond that I swim on

So next time you come through our village
Reduce your speed some more
Take note of all the pretty signs
And remember what they're for

GAS ATTAX!

Another challenging day at work and I'm looking at MSN. Found another interesting story that inspired this. Well I never!

Just when you think you've seen it all
Something new comes along
I see in Denmark they've created a tax
Based on cattle pong!

It's been worked out, a cow can emit
4 tonnes of methane a year
And this, amongst a load of other things,
That freely flows from its rear

In Denmark the farmers have to pay
80 Euros per head
In Ireland it's only 12
Depends on what they've been fed

They're trying to make a special food
Creating less gas from their flue
If that works out successfully
It'll be breakfast for me and you

2.7 tonnes of harmful CO2
Comes from the average car
But the gas coming from humans
Is known to be more lethal by far!

When I listen to my neighbour in the bath
It really is obscene
He can fart anything from Tchaikovsky's Swan Lake
To the more rousing "God Save the Queen"

He's come to a problem, when he renders the latter
To stand up takes him so long
And no one dare go in and help him do this
Without a gas mask on

For now us humans can feel assured
Will take some time to get to us
They'll probably include it in the Council Tax
Can you begin to imagine the fuss?

Gas Attax!

Slim Jim

SLIM JIM

The inspiration here is clear to see! My wife and I were moving a laurel bush from the front garden to the back! Work that one out!

Just on a whim, a guy called Jim
Decided one day he'd try to slim
He weighed in close to twenty five stone
And just standing up made him groan!

When he went for a walk, and it wasn't that far,
In fact from his front door to his car!
Jim took close on half an hour
To summon all his energy and power

You may find it strange or rather bizarre
As to how they get Jim into his car
He has a convertible and to save him pain
They lowered him in with the help of a crane

Gentleman Jim, as he was known
Took a trip up to the town
To join the health club and exercise
But that was to become his demise

When he entered the pool to have a swim
They realised nobody else could get in
Other people told the tale
Of the health club's friendly whale

Then when he went down to the gym
To lift some weights and look more trim
He couldn't quite get through the door
They had to widen it, and re-enforce the floor

The cycle seats were far too small
He sat on them and broke them all
Now he's banned from pool and gym,
And thus went his desire to slim.

PURE GENIUS

It's the 20th May 2009 and an historical event in our country's history! No you fool the Queen has already got a new flat screen telly, she got it last year! The last time this happened was, I believe, 300 years ago. Hands up who can remember it! Yes you've guessed it! The Speaker in the House of Commons has been asked to stand down. No! They're not going to re-varnish his seat, he's been sacked! To celebrate this unusual event I thought I might get away with another poem on the subject! Is that OK?

Life's in a state?
Finances too?
Then I've got the very job for you

Go into politics
It can't be beat
Particularly if you can act and cheat

There are plenty of handouts going about
And don't worry, they'll not catch you out
If they do, you say you didn't know
That'll get you off, but not "Joe public" though

Unlike you, he would go to jail
And end up pissing in a pail

Another way is to pay it back
And that will be the end of that
I know you haven't been where I have been
But it's so easy, it's obscene!

Oh! I forgot to mention
If caught, you just have to say you're sorry
Make sure your smile is at the back of the pile
On your face, a look of worry

Look very stern, like at drama school
Even though you're making a fool
Of the Taxpayer, trying to make ends meet
Three jobs, five kids and nothing to eat

If the finger of suspicion still points at you
Become a "blame" seeker
Create a gang with some of your mates
And get the resignation of the Speaker

It's all very sad to see him go,
But you don't appear to be crying
Cos you know, as well as I do
It won't stop cheating and lying!

Pure Genius

Unforgettable Love

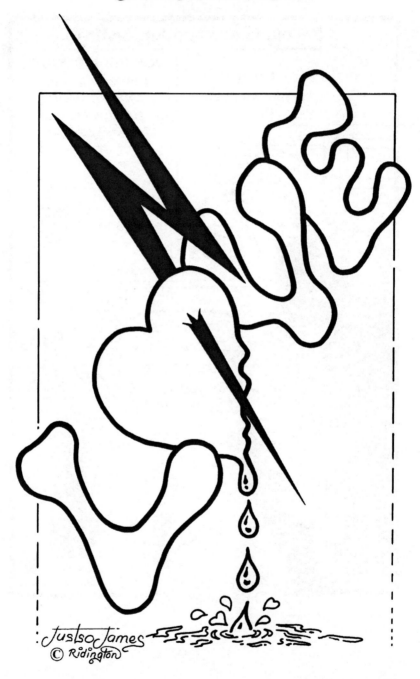

UNFORGETTABLE LOVE

How painful it must be when a relationship breaks up but one still loves the other in spite of all that's happened. Mum did Dad! It can be even more painful to see the one you love out with the new partner BUT we do have to move on, and rely on time to provide the healing touch:

When nothing is more than you deserve
And words are not enough
Four walls help me to survive
As I arrive at reality
Forgetting dreams of what might have been

Oh cruel world, full of deception
How will I rise up to face
The overwhelming truth
Of yesterday's love
When the favourite songs
That meant so much
But now when heard
Bring tears from this bruised heart
As I try to pacify
Understand why
You don't try
To conceal new love
As you wander the streets
Displaying your new trophy
With carefree abandon
Stopping to look away
Does little to reduce a pain
Like a lightening strike
Food has no place

As I seek refuge
In spirit that freely flows
To bring relief from constant suffering
But in time there's no escape
Move on, move on I hear you cry
But is love disposable
To be discarded on some rubbish tip
Along with society's failures
Tis true, it's failed
Despite many one way attempts to resurrect
But real love is a one way street
Wide enough for two

As, with eyes engaging and hands firmly held
One makes the journey of a lifetime
Of sharing and giving
World's most precious gift
The gift of love!

Lightning Source UK Ltd.
Milton Keynes UK
18 December 2010

164573UK00001B/14/P